DEPARTMENT OF THE NAVY
HEADQUARTERS UNITED STATES MARINE CORPS
3000 MARINE CORPS PENTAGON
WASHINGTON, D.C. 20350-3000

I0426304

MARINE CORPS COMMUNITY SERVICES (MCCS) TRAINING AND READINESS (T&R) MANUAL

DEPARTMENT OF THE NAVY
HEADQUARTERS UNITED STATES MARINE CORPS
3000 MARINE CORPS PENTAGON
WASHINGTON, D.C. 20350-3000

NAVMC 3500.13B
C 469

NAVMC 3500.13B

0 3 OCT 2011

From: Commandant of the Marine Corps
To: Distribution List

Subj: MARINE CORPS COMMUNITY SERVICES (MCCS) TRAINING AND READINESS (T&R)
      MANUAL

Ref: (a) MCO P3500.72A
     (b) MCO 1553.3A
     (c) MCO 3400.3F
     (d) MCO 3500.27B W/Erratum
     (e) MCRP 3-0A
     (f) MCRP 3-0B
     (g) MCO 1553.2B

1. Purpose. Per reference (a), this T&R Manual establishes required events
for standardization training of Marines and Navy personnel whose primary
mission is to carry out Marine Corps Community Services operations.
Additionally, it identifies managed on-the-job training requirements for MOS
4130 and 4133.

2. Cancellation. NAVMC 3500.13A

3. Scope

   a. Per reference (b), commanders will conduct an internal assessment of
the unit's ability to execute its mission and develop long-, mid-, and short-
range training plans to sustain proficiency and correct deficiencies.
Training plans will incorporate these events to standardize training and
provide objective assessment of progress toward attaining combat readiness.
Commanders will keep records at the unit and individual levels to record
training achievements, identify training gaps and document objective
assessments of readiness associated with training Marines. Commanders will
use reference (c) to incorporate nuclear, biological, and chemical defense
training into training plans and reference (d) to integrate operational risk
management. References (e) and (f) provide amplifying information for
effective planning and management of training within the unit.

   b. Formal school and training detachment commanders will use references
(a) and (g) to ensure programs of instruction meet skill training
requirements established in this manual, and provide career-progression
training in the events designated for initial training in the formal school
environment.

4. Information. Commanding General (CG), Training and Education Command
(TECOM) will update this T&R Manual as necessary to provide current and
relevant training standards to commanders. All questions pertaining to

the Marine Corps Ground T&R Program and Unit Training Management should be directed to: CG, TECOM (Ground Training Division C 469), 1019 Elliot Road, Quantico, VA 22134.

5. <u>Command</u>. This manual is applicable to the Marine Corps Total Force.

6. <u>Certification</u>. Reviewed and approved this date.

R. C. FOX
By direction

Distribution: PCN 10033194900

    Copy to: 7000260 (2)
              8145001 (1)

LOCATOR SHEET

Subj: MARINE CORPS COMMUNITY SERVICES (MCCS) TRAINING AND READINESS (T&R)
       MANUAL)

Location: _____

               (Indicate location(s) of copy(ies) of this Manual.)

RECORD OF CHANGES

Log completed change action as indicated

Change Number	Date of Change	Date Entered	Signature of Person Incorporating Change

MCCS T&R MANUAL

TABLE OF CONTENTS

MCCS T&R MANUAL

CHAPTER 1

OVERVIEW

MCCS T&R MANUAL

CHAPTER 1

OVERVIEW

1000. INTRODUCTION

1. The T&R Program is the Corps' primary tool for planning, conducting and evaluating training, and assessing training readiness. Subject matter experts (SMEs) from the operating forces developed core capability Mission Essential Task Lists (METLs) for ground communities derived from the Marine Corps Task List (MCTL). T&R Manuals are built around these METLs and all events contained in T&R Manuals relate directly to this METL. This comprehensive T&R Program will help to ensure the Marine Corps continues to improve its combat readiness by training more efficiently and effectively. Ultimately, this will enhance the Marine Corps' ability to accomplish real-world missions.

2. The T&R Manual contains the individual and collective training requirements to prepare units to accomplish their combat mission. The T&R Manual is not intended to be an encyclopedia that contains every minute detail of how to accomplish training. Instead, it identifies the minimum standards that Marines must be able to perform in combat. The T&R Manual is a fundamental tool for commanders to build and maintain unit combat readiness. Using this tool, leaders can construct and execute an effective training plan that supports the unit's METL. More detailed information on the Marine Corps Ground T&R Program is found in reference (a).

1001. UNIT TRAINING

1. The training of Marines to perform as an integrated unit in combat lies at the heart of the T&R program. Unit and individual readiness are directly related. Individual training and the mastery of individual core skills serve as the building blocks for unit combat readiness. A Marine's ability to perform critical skills required in combat is essential. However, it is not necessary to have all individuals within a unit fully trained in order for that organization to accomplish its assigned tasks. Manpower shortfalls, temporary assignments, leave, or other factors outside the commander's control, often affect the ability to conduct individual training. During these periods, unit readiness is enhanced if emphasis is placed on the individual training of Marines on-hand. Subsequently, these Marines will be mission ready and capable of executing as part of a team when the full complement of personnel is available.

2. Commanders will ensure that all training is focused on their combat mission. The T&R Manual is a tool to help develop the unit's training plan. In most cases, unit training should focus on achieving unit proficiency in the core capabilities METL. However, commanders will adjust their training focus to support METLs associated with a major OPLAN/CONPLAN or named operation as designated by their higher commander and reported accordingly in the Defense Readiness Reporting System (DRRS). Training will support the

METL in use by the commander and be tailored to meet T&R standards. Commanders at all levels are responsible for effective combat training. The conduct of training in a professional manner consistent with Marine Corps standards cannot be over emphasized.

3. Commanders will provide personnel the opportunity to attend formal and operational level courses of instruction as required by this Manual. Attendance at all formal courses must enhance the warfighting capabilities of the unit as determined by the unit commander.

1002. UNIT TRAINING MANAGEMENT

1. Unit Training Management (UTM) is the application of the Systems Approach to Training (SAT) and the Marine Corps Training Principles. This is accomplished in a manner that maximizes training results and focuses the training priorities of the unit in preparation for the conduct of its wartime mission.

2. UTM techniques, described in references (b) and (e), provide commanders with the requisite tools and techniques to analyze, design, develop, implement, and evaluate the training of their unit. The Marine Corps Training Principles, explained in reference (b), provide sound and proven direction and are flexible enough to accommodate the demands of local conditions. These principles are not inclusive, nor do they guarantee success. They are guides that commanders can use to manage unit-training programs. The Marine Corps training principles are:

- Train as you fight
- Make commanders responsible for training
- Use standards-based training
- Use performance-oriented training
- Use mission-oriented training
- Train the MAGTF to fight as a combined arms team
- Train to sustain proficiency
- Train to challenge

3. To maintain an efficient and effective training program, leaders at every level must understand and implement UTM. Guidance for UTM and the process for establishing effective programs are contained in references (a) through (g).

1003. SUSTAINMENT AND EVALUATION OF TRAINING

1. The evaluation of training is necessary to properly prepare Marines for combat. Evaluations are either formal or informal, and performed by members of the unit (internal evaluation) or from an external command (external evaluation).

2. Marines are expected to maintain proficiency in the training events for their MOS at the appropriate grade or billet to which assigned. Leaders are responsible for recording the training achievements of their Marines. Whether it involves individual or collective training events, they must ensure proficiency is sustained by requiring retraining of each event at or

before expiration of the designated sustainment interval. Performance of the training event, however, is not sufficient to ensure combat readiness. Leaders at all levels must evaluate the performance of their Marines and the unit as they complete training events, and only record successful accomplishment of training based upon the evaluation. The goal of evaluation is to ensure that correct methods are employed to achieve the desired standard, or the Marines understand how they need to improve in order to attain the standard. Leaders must determine whether credit for completing a training event is recorded if the standard was not achieved. While successful accomplishment is desired, debriefing of errors can result in successful learning that will allow ethical recording of training event completion. Evaluation is a continuous process that is integral to training management and is conducted by leaders at every level and during all phases of planning and the conduct of training. To ensure training is efficient and effective, evaluation is an integral part of the training plan. Ultimately, leaders remain responsible for determining if the training was effective.

3. The purpose of formal and informal evaluation is to provide commanders with a process to determine a unit's/Marine's proficiency in the tasks that must be performed in combat. Informal evaluations are conducted during every training evolution. Formal evaluations are often scenario-based, focused on the unit's METs, based on collective training standards, and usually conducted during higher-level collective events. References (a) and (f) provide further guidance on the conduct of informal and formal evaluations using the Marine Corps Ground T&R Program.

1004. ORGANIZATION

1. The Marine Corps Community Services T&R Manual is a community-based manual, written to support the MCCS community. The manual is not intended, nor should it be used as a stand-alone document. The manual is organized in five chapters.

   a. Chapter 1 is an overview of the Marine Corps's Training and Readiness program. It consists of elements common to all MOSs that are pertinent to successful implementation of a Training and Readiness program. Chapter 1 also outlines the organization and key elements of the MCCS T&R Manual, with explanations of each key element.

   b. Chapters 2 and 3 consist of the Mission Essential Tasks and collective training events for the MCCS community. Collective Training Events are arranged by event code under the appropriate supported MET. An index of collective events arranged by level is included for easy referencing.

   c. Chapters 4 and 5 consist of the Individual Training Events for the Marine Corps Community Services Officer (4130 MOS) and the Marine Corps Community Services Marine (4133 MOS). Events are arranged by MOS/EVENT CODE. An index of the individual events arranged by level is included in each chapter for easy referencing.

1005. T&R EVENT CODING. T&R events are coded for ease of reference. Each event has a 4-4-4-digit identifier. The first four digits represent either the Community or the MOS (4130 or 4133). The second four digits represent the functional or duty area (Contracts/Contracting Services (CONT), Expeditionary (EXPD), Financial Management (FMGT), Management (MGMT), and Operations (OPS). The last four digits represent the level and sequence of the event. The T&R levels are shown in figure (1). An example of the T&R coding used in this manual is shown in figure (2).

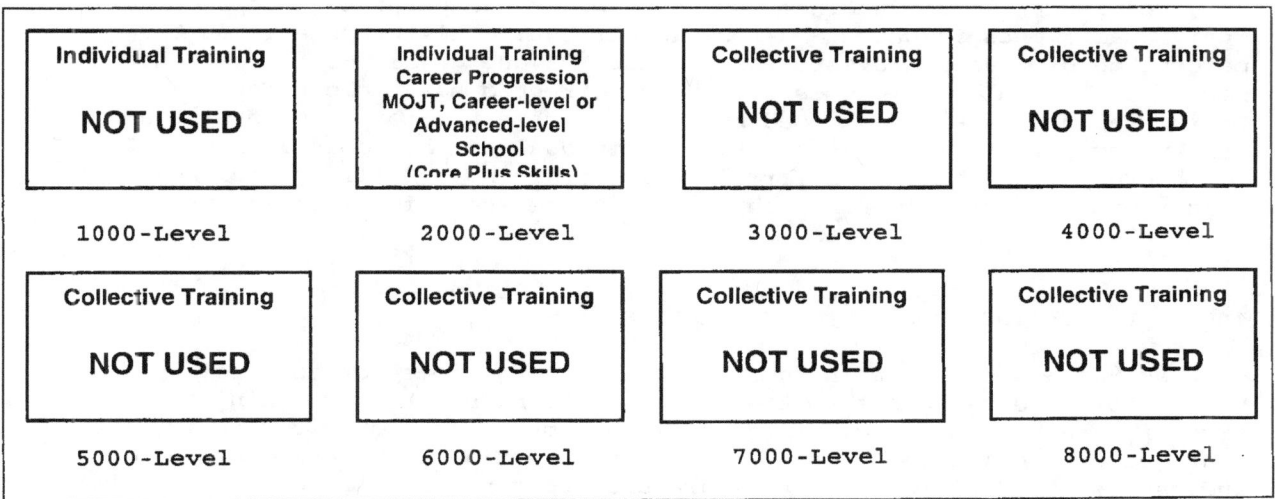

Figure 1: T&R Event Levels

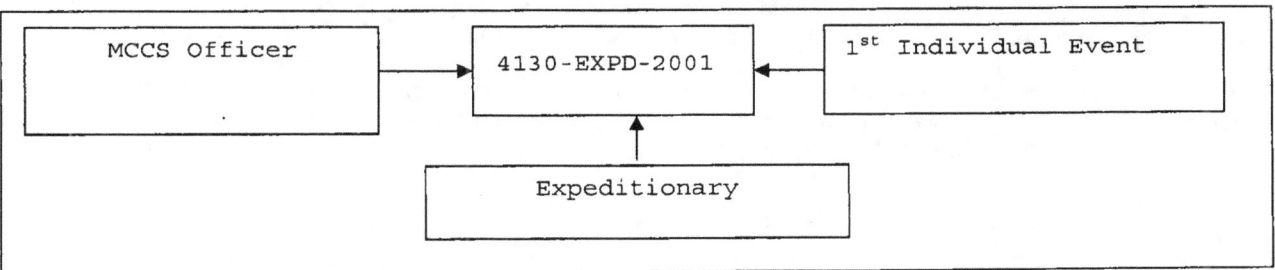

Figure 2: T&R Event Coding

1006. COMBAT READINESS PERCENTAGE

1. The Marine Corps Ground T&R Program includes processes to assess readiness of units and individual Marines. Every unit in the Marine Corps maintains a basic level of readiness based on the training and experience of the Marines in the unit. Even units that never trained together are capable of accomplishing some portion of their missions. Combat readiness assessment does not associate a quantitative value for this baseline of readiness, but uses a "Combat Readiness Percentage", as a method to provide a concise descriptor of the recent training accomplishments of units and Marines.

2. Combat Readiness Percentage (CRP) is the percentage of required training events that a unit or Marine accomplishes within specified sustainment intervals.

3. Combat readiness is assessed as a percentage of the successfully completed and current (within sustainment interval) key training events called "Evaluation-Coded" (E-Coded) Events. E-Coded Events and unit CRP calculation are described in follow-on paragraphs. CRP achieved through the completion of E-Coded Events is directly relevant to readiness assessment in DRRS.

4. Individual combat readiness is assessed as the percentage of required individual events in which a Marine is current. This translates as the percentage of training events for his/her MOS and grade (or billet) that the Marine successfully completes within the directed sustainment interval. Individual skills are developed through a combination of 1000-level training (entry-level formal school courses), individual on-the-job training in 2000-level events, and follow-on formal school training. Skill proficiency is maintained by retraining in each event per the specified sustainment interval.

1007. EVALUATION-CODED (E-CODED) EVENTS

1. T&R Manuals can contain numerous unit events, some for the whole unit and others for integral parts that serve as building blocks for training. To simplify training management and readiness assessment, only collective events that are critical components of a mission essential task (MET), or key indicators of a unit's readiness, are used to generate CRP for a MET. These critical or key events are designated in the T&R Manual as Evaluation-Coded (E-Coded) events. Formal evaluation of unit performance in these events is recommended because of their value in assessing combat readiness. Only E-Coded events are used to calculate CRP for each MET.

2. The use of a METL-based training program allows the commander discretion in training. This makes the T&R Manual a training tool rather than a prescriptive checklist.

1008. CRP CALCULATION

1. Collective training begins at the 3000 level (tactical, team, crew or equivalent). Unit training plans are designed to accomplish the events that support the unit METL while simultaneously sustaining proficiency in individual core skills. These collective events are E-Coded and the only events that contribute to unit CRP. This is done to assist commanders in prioritizing the training toward the METL, taking into account resource, time, and personnel constraints.

2. Unit CRP increases after the completion of E-Coded events. The number of E-Coded events for the MET determines the value of each E-Coded event. For example, if there are 4 E-Coded events for a MET, each is worth 25% of MET CRP. MET CRP is calculated by adding the percentage of each completed and current (within sustainment interval) E-Coded training event. The percentage for each MET is calculated the same way and all are added together and divided by the number of METS to determine unit CRP. For ease of calculation, we will say that each MET has 4 E-Coded events, each contributing 25% towards the completion of the MET. If the unit has completed and is current on three of the four E-Coded events for a given MET,

then they have completed 75% of the MET. The CRP for each MET is added together and divided by the number of METS to get unit CRP; unit CRP is the average of MET CRP.

For Example:

MET 1: 75% complete (3 of 4 E-Coded events trained)
MET 2: 100% complete (6 of 6 E-Coded events trained)
MET 3: 25% complete (1 of 4 E-Coded events trained)
MET 4: 50% complete (2 of 4 E-Coded events trained)
MET 5: 75% complete (3 of 4 E-Coded events trained)

To get unit CRP, simply add the CRP for each MET and divide by the number of METS:

MET CRP: 75 + 100 + 25 + 50 + 75 = 325

Unit CRP: 325 (total MET CRP)/5 (total number of METS) = 65%

1009. T&R EVENT COMPOSITION

1. This section explains each of the components of a T&R event. These items are included in all events in each T&R Manual.

    a. Event Code (see Sect 1006). The event code is a 4-4-4 character set. For individual training events, the first 4 characters indicate the occupational function. The second 4 characters indicate functional area (ADOP, LOAD, RIG, etc.). The third 4 characters are simply a numerical designator for the event.

    b. Event Title. The event title is the name of the event.

    c. E-Coded. This is a "yes/no" category to indicate whether or not the event is E-Coded. If yes, the event contributes toward the CRP of the associated MET. The value of each E-Coded event is based on number of E-Coded events for that MET. Refer to paragraph 1008 for detailed explanation of E-Coded events.

    d. Supported MET(s). List all METs that are supported by the training event.

    e. Sustainment Interval. This is the period, expressed in number of months, between evaluation or retraining requirements. Skills and capabilities acquired through the accomplishment of training events are refreshed at pre-determined intervals. It is essential that these intervals are adhered to in order to ensure Marines maintain proficiency.

    f. Billet. Individual training events may contain a list of billets within the community that are responsible for performing that event. This ensures that the billet's expected tasks are clearly articulated and a Marine's readiness to perform in that billet is measured.

    g. Grade. Each individual training event will list the rank(s) at which Marines are required to learn and sustain the training event.

h. <u>Event Description</u>. Provide a description of the event purpose, objectives, goals, and requirements. It is a general description of an action requiring learned skills and knowledge (e.g. Conduct immediate action against a convoy ambush).

i. <u>Condition</u>. Describe the condition(s), under which tasks are performed. Conditions are based on a "real world" operational environment. They indicate what is provided (equipment, materials, manuals, aids, etc.), environmental constraints, conditions under which the task is performed, and any specific cues or indicators to which the performer must respond. When resources or safety requirements limit the conditions, this is stated.

j. <u>Standard</u>. The standard indicates the basis for judging effectiveness of the performance. It consists of a carefully worded statement that identifies the proficiency level expected when the task is performed. The standard provides the minimum acceptable performance parameters and is strictly adhered to. The standard for collective events is general, describing the desired end-state or purpose of the event. While the standard for individual events specifically describe to what proficiency level in terms of accuracy, speed, sequencing, quality of performance, adherence to procedural guidelines, etc., the event is accomplished.

k. <u>Event Components</u>. Describe the actions composing the event and help the user determine what must be accomplished and to properly plan for the event.

l. <u>Prerequisite Events</u>. Prerequisites are academic training or other T&R events that must be completed prior to attempting the task. They are lower-level events or tasks that give the individual/unit the skills required to accomplish the event. They can also be planning steps, administrative requirements, or specific parameters that build toward mission accomplishment.

m. <u>Chained Events</u>. Collective T&R events are supported by lower-level collective and individual T&R events. This enables unit leaders to effectively identify subordinate T&R events that ultimately support specific mission essential tasks. When the accomplishment of any upper-level events, by their nature, result in the performance of certain subordinate and related events, the events are "chained." The completion of chained events will update sustainment interval credit (and CRP for E-Coded events) for the related subordinate level events.

n. <u>Related Events</u>. Provide a list of all Individual Training Standards that support the event.

o. <u>References</u>. The training references are utilized to determine task performance steps, grading criteria, and ensure standardization of training procedures. They assist the trainee in satisfying the performance standards, or the trainer in evaluating the effectiveness of task completion. References are also important to the development of detailed training plans.

p. <u>Distance Learning Products</u> (IMI, CBT, MCI, etc.). Include this component when the event can be taught via one of these media methods vice attending a formal course of instruction or receiving MOJT.

q. <u>Support Requirements</u>. This is a list of the external and internal support the unit and Marines will need to complete the event. The list includes, but is not limited to:

- Range(s)/Training Area
- Ordnance
- Equipment
- Materials
- Other Units/Personnel
- Other Support Requirements

r. <u>Miscellaneous</u>. Provide any additional information that assists in the planning and execution of the event. Miscellaneous information may include. but is not limited to:

- Admin Instructions
- Special Personnel Certifications
- Equipment Operating Hours
- Road Miles

1010. CBRNE TRAINING

1. All personnel assigned to the operating force must be trained in chemical, biological, radiological, and nuclear defense (CBRND), in order to survive and continue their mission in a CBRN environment. Individual proficiency standards are defined as survival and basic operating standards. Survival standards are those that the individual must master in order to survive a CBRN incident. Basic operating standards are those that the individual, and collectively the unit, must perform to continue operations in a CBRNE environment.

2. CBRN Officers and Specialists are instrumental in integrating realistic scenarios/situations that challenge units' ability to operate in a CBRN environment. Units should train under CBRNE conditions whenever possible. Per reference (c), all units must be capable of accomplishing their assigned mission in a contaminated environment.

1011. NIGHT TRAINING

1. While it is understood that all personnel and units of the operating force are capable of performing their assigned mission in "every climate and place," current doctrine emphasizes the requirement to perform assigned missions at night and during periods of limited visibility. Basic skills are significantly more difficult when visibility is limited.

2. To ensure units are capable of accomplishing their mission they must train under the conditions of limited visibility. Units should strive to conduct all events in this T&R Manual during both day and night/limited visibility conditions. When there is limited training time available, night training should take precedence over daylight training, contingent on individual, crew, and unit proficiency.

1012. OPERATIONAL RISK MANAGEMENT (ORM)

1. ORM is a process that enables commanders to plan for and minimize risk while still accomplishing the mission. It is a decision making tool used by Marines at all levels to increase operational effectiveness by anticipating hazards and reducing the potential for loss, thereby increasing the probability of a successful mission. ORM minimizes risks to acceptable levels, commensurate with mission accomplishment.

2. Commanders, leaders, maintainers, planners, and schedulers will integrate risk assessment in the decision-making process and implement hazard controls to reduce risk to acceptable levels. Applying the ORM process will reduce mishaps, lower costs, and provide for more efficient use of resources. ORM assists the commander in conserving lives and resources and avoiding unnecessary risk, making an informed decision to implement a course of action (COA), identifying feasible and effective control measures where specific measures do not exist, and providing reasonable alternatives for mission accomplishment. Most importantly, ORM assists the commander in determining the balance between training realism and unnecessary risks in training, the impact of training operations on the environment, and the adjustment of training plans to fit the level of proficiency and experience of Sailors/Marines and leaders. Further guidance for ORM is found in references (b) and (d).

1013. MARINE CORPS GROUND T&R PROGRAM

1. The Marine Corps Ground T&R Program continues to evolve. The vision for Ground T&R Program is to publish a T&R Manual for every readiness-reporting unit so that core capability METs are clearly defined with supporting collective training standards, and to publish community-based T&R Manuals for all occupational fields whose personnel augment other units to increase their combat and/or logistic capabilities. The vision for this program includes plans to provide a Marine Corps training management information system that enables tracking of unit and individual training accomplishments by unit commanders and small unit leaders, automatically computing CRP for both units and individual Marines based upon MOS and rank (or billet). Linkage of T&R Events to the Marine Corps Task List (MCTL), through the core capability METs, has enabled objective assessment of training readiness in the DRRS.

2. DRRS measures and reports on the readiness of military forces and the supporting infrastructure to meet missions and goals assigned by the Secretary of Defense. With unit CRP based on the unit's training toward its METs, the CRP will provide a more accurate picture of a unit's readiness. This will give fidelity to future funding requests and factor into the allocation of resources. Additionally, the Ground T&R Program will help to ensure training remains focused on mission accomplishment and that training readiness reporting is tied to units' METLs.

MCCS T&R MANUAL

CHAPTER 2

MISSION ESSENTIAL TASKS MATRIX

This chapter remains as a placeholder for future use.

MCCS T&R MANUAL

CHAPTER 3

COLLECTIVE EVENTS

This chapter remains as a placeholder for future use.

MCCS T&R MANUAL

CHAPTER 4

MOS 4130 INDIVIDUAL EVENTS

CHAPTER 4

MOS 4130 INDIVIDUAL EVENTS

4000. PURPOSE. This chapter contains individual training events for the Marine Corps Community services Officer.

4001. EVENT CODING. Events in the T&R Manual are depicted with an up to 12 field alphanumeric system, i.e. XXXX-XXXX-XXXX. This chapter utilizes the following methodology:

a. Field one. Each event starts with 4130, indicating that the event is for MOS 4130, Marine Corps Community Services Officer.

b. Field two. This field is alpha characters indicating a functional area. In this chapter, the functional areas are as follows:

Code	Description	Example
CONT	Contracting/Contracting Services	4130-CONT-XXXX
EXPD	Expeditionary Operations	4130-EXPD-XXXX
FMGT	Financial Management	4130-FMGT-XXXX
MGMT	Basic Management	4130-MGMT-XXXX
OPS	Business Operations	4130-OPS-XXXX

c. Field three. All individual events within T&R Manuals are either 1000-level for events taught at MOS-producing formal schools or 2000-level for events taught at advanced-level schools or MOJT. This chapter contains only 2000-level events.

4002. INITIAL TRAINING SETTING. The tasks marked "Formal School" in this manual refer to Civilian establishments. The Marine Corps Community Services MOS does not currently have military training schools. Officer and Enlisted personnel must attend civilian establishments to attain the qualifications and certifications they require to perform certain duties. A list of required and recommended training is provided in Appendix A.

4003. INDEX OF INDIVIDUAL EVENTS

Event Code	Event	Page
	2000-LEVEL	
4130-CONT-2101	Write a statement of work	4-4
4130-CONT-2102	Submit a request for proposals	4-4
4130-CONT-2103	Award contracts	4-5
4130-EXPD-2201	Plan expeditionary operations	4-5
4130-EXPD-2202	Develop MCCS appendix to operation order	4-6
4130-EXPD-2203	Develop Standard Operating Procedures (SOP) for MCCS field activities	4-6
4130-EXPD-2204	Direct establishment of MCCS field facilities	4-7
4130-EXPD-2205	Develop retrograde procedures for MCCS Field Facility	4-7
4130-EXPD-2206	Implement expansion/renovation program	4-8
4130-EXPD-2207	Analyze patron surveys	4-9
4130-EXPD-2208	Develop a marketing action plan	4-9
4130-EXPD-2209	Prepare merchandise plan	4-10
4130-FMGT-2301	Establish cash custody procedure	4-10
4130-FMGT-2302	Analyze performance of retail operations	4-11
4130-FMGT-2303	Request Appropriated Fund (APF) support	4-11
4130-MGMT-2401	Monitor MCCS Hazardous Materials (HAZMAT) merchandise	4-12
4130-MGMT-2402	Evaluate a merchandise presentation	4-12
4130-OPS-2501	Review customer satisfaction programs	4-13
4130-OPS-2502	Monitor special events	4-13
4130-OPS-2503	Evaluate a marketing action plan	4-14
4130-OPS-2504	Examine asset protection program	4-14
4130-OPS-2505	Monitor inventories	4-15
4130-OPS-2506	Review MCCS Safety/Health/Environmental Program	4-15
4130-OPS-2507	Monitor food and beverage operations	4-16
4130-OPS-2508	Review SERVSAFE program	4-16

4004. 2000-LEVEL EVENTS

4130-CONT-2101: Write a statement of work

EVALUATION-CODED: NO   **SUSTAINMENT INTERVAL:** 12 months

GRADES: WO-1, CWO-2, CWO-3, CWO-4, CWO-5

INITIAL TRAINING SETTING: FORMAL

CONDITION: Given the needs for equipment, supplies, services, concessionaires or entertainment.

STANDARD: Ensuring MCCS goods and services are procured.

PERFORMANCE STEPS:
1. Conduct business analysis.
2. Conduct market research.
3. Specify contract deliverables.
4. Write single or sole source justification memorandum

REFERENCES:
1. DOD 5500.7-R Joint Ethics Regulation (JER)
2. DODI 1015.10 Programs for Military Morale, Welfare, and Recreation (MWR)
3. DODI 4105.71 Nonappropriated Fund (NAF) Procurement
4. MCO P7010.20 Marine Corps Community Services Nonappropriated Fund Procurement Policy

---

4130-CONT-2102: Submit a request for proposals

EVALUATION-CODED: NO   **SUSTAINMENT INTERVAL:** 12 months

GRADES: WO-1, CWO-2, CWO-3, CWO-4, CWO-5

INITIAL TRAINING SETTING: FORMAL

CONDITION: Given the need for equipment, supplies, services, concessionaires or entertainment.

STANDARD: Obtaining competitive offers for MCCS goods and services.

PERFORMANCE STEPS:
1. Receive procurement request and review for completeness.
2. Select appropriate contract vehicle for procurement action.
3. Create a source list including any mandatory sources.
4. Prepare request for quotes or request for proposals.
5. Conduct pre-proposal or pre-award meetings as necessary.

REFERENCES:
1. DOD 5500.7-R Joint Ethics Regulation (JER)
2. DODI 1015.10 Programs for Military Morale, Welfare, and Recreation (MWR)
3. DODI 4105.71 Nonappropriated Fund (NAF) Procurement

4. MCO P1700.27B Marine Corps Community Services Policy Manual
5. MCO P7010.20 Marine Corps Community Services Nonappropriated Fund
    Procurement Policy

4130-CONT-2103: Award contracts

EVALUATION-CODED: NO   **SUSTAINMENT INTERVAL:** 12 months

DESCRIPTION: Statement of work and RFP must be completed before this task can occur.

GRADES: WO-1, CWO-2, CWO-3, CWO-4, CWO-5

INITIAL TRAINING SETTING: FORMAL

CONDITION: Given the need.

STANDARD: Ensuring MCCS contracts are granted in compliance with MCO 7010.20.

PERFORMANCE STEPS:
1. Evaluate proposals.
2. Conduct negotiations.
3. Determine contractor responsibility.
4. Use purchase card when appropriate.
5. Notify interested parties of award determination.
6. Appoint Contracting Officer's Representative when appropriate.
7. Conduct post-award meetings.

REFERENCES:
1. DOD 5500.7-R Joint Ethics Regulation (JER)
2. DODI 1015.10 Programs for Military Morale, Welfare, and Recreation (MWR)
3. DODI 4105.71 Nonappropriated Fund (NAF) Procurement
4. MCO P7010.20 Marine Corps Community Services Nonappropriated Fund
    Procurement Policy

MISCELLANEOUS:

   ADMINISTRATIVE INSTRUCTIONS: Only warranted NAF contracting officials may award contracts.

4130-EXPD-2201: Plan expeditionary operations

EVALUATION-CODED: NO   **SUSTAINMENT INTERVAL:** 12 months

GRADES: WO-1, CWO-2, CWO-3, CWO-4, CWO-5

INITIAL TRAINING SETTING: MOJT

CONDITION: Given a projected mission.

STANDARD: Ensuring MCCS support is available to accommodate all personnel.

PERFORMANCE STEPS:
1. Determine number of personnel to be supported.
2. Determine duration of operation.
3. Identify number of personnel for staffing.
4. Establish assortment/equipment.
5. Determine source of supply.
6. Determine external support requirements.
7. Request appropriate structures.

REFERENCES:
1. MCO P1700.27B Marine Corps Community Services Policy Manual
2. MCO P1700.30 Marine Corps Community Services Business Operations Manual
3. MCWP 4-11.8 Services in an Expeditionary Environment

4130-EXPD-2202: Develop MCCS appendix to operation order

EVALUATION-CODED: NO   **SUSTAINMENT INTERVAL:** 12 months

GRADES: WO-1, CWO-2, CWO-3, CWO-4, CWO-5

INITIAL TRAINING SETTING: FORMAL

CONDITION: Given commander's intent.

STANDARD: Ensuring all requirements are identified.

PERFORMANCE STEPS:
1. Verify the mission to include the commander's intent.
2. Verify the overall concept of operation.
3. Determine supportability.
4. Analyze the situation, mission, execution, administration and logistics, and command and control.
5. Develop a draft.

REFERENCES:
1. MCO P1700.27B Marine Corps Community Services Policy Manual
2. MCWP 4-11.8 Services in an Expeditionary Environment

4130-EXPD-2203: Develop Standard Operating Procedures (SOP) for MCCS field activities

EVALUATION-CODED: NO   **SUSTAINMENT INTERVAL:** 12 months

GRADES: WO-1, CWO-2, CWO-3, CWO-4, CWO-5

INITIAL TRAINING SETTING: FORMAL

CONDITION: In an Expeditionary environment, given publications, Table of Organization & Equipment (TO&E), directives, personnel, administrative equipment and references.

STANDARD: Ensuring operating procedures, administration, and accounting are performed daily.

PERFORMANCE STEPS:
1. Identify the activity.
2. Define operating procedures.
3. Review for compliance with orders and regulations.
4. Establish desktop procedures.

REFERENCES:
1. JP 3-07.5 Noncombatant Evacuation Operations
2. MCO P1700.27B Marine Corps Community Services Policy Manual
3. MCO P1700.30 Marine Corps Community Services Business Operations Manual
4. MCWP 4-1 Logistics Operations
5. MCWP 4-11 Tactical-Level Logistics
6. MCWP 4-11.8 Services in an Expeditionary Environment

4130-EXPD-2204: Direct establishment of MCCS field facilities

EVALUATION-CODED: NO   **SUSTAINMENT INTERVAL:** 12 months

GRADES: WO-1, CWO-2, CWO-3, CWO-4, CWO-5

INITIAL TRAINING SETTING: MOJT

CONDITION: Given a requirement.

STANDARD: Ensuring that space, assets and personnel requirements are adequate to meet the mission.

PERFORMANCE STEPS:
1. Validate number of personnel for staffing.
2. Determine duration of operation.
3. Request appropriate structures.

REFERENCES:
1. DODI 1015.10 Programs for Military Morale, Welfare, and Recreation (MWR)
2. DoDD 1015.2 Military Morale, Welfare and Recreation
3. JP 1-0 Personnel Support to Joint Operations
4. MCO P1700.27B Marine Corps Community Services Policy Manual
5. MCO P1700.29 Marine Corps Semper Fit Program Manual
6. MCO P1700.30 Marine Corps Community Services Business Operations Manual
7. MCWP 4-11.8 Services in an Expeditionary Environment

4130-EXPD-2205: Develop retrograde procedures for MCCS field facility

EVALUATION-CODED: NO   **SUSTAINMENT INTERVAL:** 12 months

GRADES: WO-1, CWO-2, CWO-3, CWO-4, CWO-5

INITIAL TRAINING SETTING: MOJT

CONDITION: When activities are no longer required.

STANDARD: Ensuring all assets are accounted for.

PERFORMANCE STEPS:
1. Direct inventory of all assets.
2. Ensure negotiable instruments are secured.
3. Obtain a list of all assets.
4. Arrange logistical support for embarkation.

REFERENCES:
1. DODI 1015.10 Programs for Military Morale, Welfare, and Recreation (MWR)
2. DoDD 1015.2 Military Morale, Welfare and Recreation
3. JP 1-0 Personnel Support to Joint Operations
4. MCO P1700.27B Marine Corps Community Services Policy Manual
5. MCO P1700.29 Marine Corps Semper Fit Program Manual
6. MCWP 4-1 Logistics Operations
7. MCWP 4-11 Tactical-Level Logistics

4130-EXPD-2206: Develop expansion/renovation program

EVALUATION-CODED: NO   SUSTAINMENT INTERVAL: 12 months

DESCRIPTION: Recommendations and justification to acquire funding for construction of new facilities or expansion/renovation of existing facilities is the focus of this task.

GRADES: WO-1, CWO-2, CWO-3, CWO-4, CWO-5

INITIAL TRAINING SETTING: MOJT

CONDITION: Given the need to change or upgrade existing facilities.

STANDARD: Ensuring that requirements are funded and equipped to meet determined needs.

PERFORMANCE STEPS:
1. Determine appropriate scope of project.
2. Provide usage data and/or letter of justification.
3. Determine funding method and availability.

REFERENCES:
1. DODI 1015.10 Programs for Military Morale, Welfare, and Recreation (MWR)
2. DODI 1015.14 Establishment, Management, and Control of Nonappropriated Fund Instrumentalities and Financial Management of Supporting Resources
3. DoDD 1015.2 Military Morale, Welfare and Recreation
4. JP 1-0 Personnel Support to Joint Operations
5. MCO P1700.27B Marine Corps Community Services Policy Manual

6. MCO P1700.29 Marine Corps Semper Fit Program Manual
7. MCO P1700.30 Marine Corps Community Services Business Operations Manual

---

4130-EXPD-2207: Direct patron surveys

EVALUATION-CODED: NO   **SUSTAINMENT INTERVAL:** 12 months

GRADES: WO-1, CWO-2, CWO-3, CWO-4, CWO-5

INITIAL TRAINING SETTING: MOJT

CONDITION: Given MCCS operations and customer base.

STANDARD: Identifying all deficiencies and make operational changes.

PERFORMANCE STEPS:
1. Prepare or contract survey.
2. Analyze survey.
3. Order operational changes.

REFERENCES:
1. DODI 1015.10 Programs for Military Morale, Welfare, and Recreation (MWR)
2. DODI 1015.14 Establishment, Management, and Control of Nonappropriated Fund Instrumentalities and Financial Management of Supporting Resources
3. DODI 4105.71 Nonappropriated Fund (NAF) Procurement
4. DoDD 1015.2 Military Morale, Welfare and Recreation
5. DoDD 4105.67 Nonappropriated Fund (NAF) Procurement Policy
6. JP 1-0 Personnel Support to Joint Operations
7. MCO P1700.27B Marine Corps Community Services Policy Manual
8. MCO P1700.29 Marine Corps Semper Fit Program Manual
9. MCO P1700.30 Marine Corps Community Services Business Operations Manual
10. MCO P7010.20 Marine Corps Community Services Nonappropriated Fund Procurement Policy

---

4130-EXPD-2208: Develop a marketing action plan

EVALUATION-CODED: NO   **SUSTAINMENT INTERVAL:** 12 months

GRADES: WO-1, CWO-2, CWO-3, CWO-4, CWO-5

INITIAL TRAINING SETTING: MOJT

CONDITION: Given the need, existing troop strength and potential.

STANDARD: Increasing patronage and awareness of MCCS goods and services.

PERFORMANCE STEPS:
1. Solicit suggestions.
2. Identify events.
3. Establish advertising procedures.
4. Direct plan.

REFERENCES:
1. MCO P1700.27B Marine Corps Community Services Policy Manual

---

4130-EXPD-2209: Prepare merchandise plan

EVALUATION-CODED: NO   **SUSTAINMENT INTERVAL:** 12 months

GRADES: WO-1, CWO-2, CWO-3, CWO-4, CWO-5

INITIAL TRAINING SETTING: MOJT

CONDITION: In a deployed environment given historical data and forecasted troop strength.

STANDARD: Ensuring merchandise meets customer demand.

PERFORMANCE STEPS:
1. Analyze previous sales data/history.
2. Determine funding available.
3. Project future sales.
4. Determine profitability of departments.

REFERENCES:
1. MCO 10123.8 Commercially Procured Marine Corps Uniforms and Accessories Sold Through Marine Corps Exchanges
2. MCO P1700.27B Marine Corps Community Services Policy Manual
3. MCO P1700.30 Marine Corps Community Services Business Operations Manual

---

4130-FMGT-2301: Establish cash custody procedure

EVALUATION-CODED: NO   **SUSTAINMENT INTERVAL:** 12 months

GRADES: WO-1, CWO-2, CWO-3, CWO-4, CWO-5

INITIAL TRAINING SETTING: MOJT

CONDITION: In a MCCS environment, given the need for an Operational Change Fund and the references.

STANDARD: To ensure accountability and proper safeguard of funds.

PERFORMANCE STEPS:
1. Obtain funds.
2. Provide guidance to individuals on proper cash handling procedures.
3. Issue funds and have Custody Receipts signed or updated.
4. Ensure deposits are submitted timely and accurately.
5. Ensure handling of Negotiable Instruments.
6. Conduct random safe and register counts/audits.

REFERENCES:
1. DoD 7000.14-R DoD Financial Management Regulation (DoDFMR), Volume 7A

2. MCO P1700.27B Marine Corps Community Services Policy Manual
3. MCO P4066.17 Marine Corps Exchange Security and Loss Prevention Manual
    (May 82)
4. MCWP 4-11.8 Services in an Expeditionary Environment

4130-FMGT-2302: Analyze performance of retail operations

EVALUATION-CODED: NO   **SUSTAINMENT INTERVAL:** 12 months

DESCRIPTION: This task requires you to compute Gross Margin Return on Investment (GMROI), Gross Margin Return on Labor (GMROL), and Gross Margin Return on Square Footage (GMROF).

GRADES: WO-1, CWO-2, CWO-3, CWO-4, CWO-5

INITIAL TRAINING SETTING: FORMAL

CONDITION: Given historical financial data.

STANDARD: Ensuring calculated Gross Margin Return on Investment, Labor & Square Footage meet criteria in MCO 1700.30.

PERFORMANCE STEPS:
1. Determine matrix.
2. Input data into appropriate matrix.
3. Analyze data.
4. Determine if established MCCS standards are met.
5. Make changes in operation, as required.

REFERENCES:
1. DoD 7000.14-R DoD Financial Management Regulation (DoDFMR), Volume 7A
2. MCO P1700.27B Marine Corps Community Services Policy Manual
3. MCO P1700.30 Marine Corps Community Services Business Operations Manual
4. MCO P4066.17 Marine Corps Exchange Security and Loss Prevention Manual
    (May 82)
5. MCWP 4-11.8 Services in an Expeditionary Environment

4130-FMGT-2303: Request Appropriated Fund (APF) support

EVALUATION-CODED: NO   **SUSTAINMENT INTERVAL:** 12 months

INITIAL TRAINING SETTING: MOJT

CONDITION: Given the contractual requirement for an official command function.

STANDARD: Ensuring MCCS facilities are reimbursed.

PERFORMANCE STEPS:
1. Identify the requirement.
2. Review contractual agreement.

3. Gather financial data.
4. Submit the appropriate documentation/request for reimbursement.

REFERENCES:
1. DoD 7000.14-R DoD Financial Management Regulation (DoDFMR), Volume 7A
2. MCO P1700.27B Marine Corps Community Services Policy Manual

3. MCO P4066.17 Marine Corps Exchange Security and Loss Prevention Manual (May 82)
4. MCWP 4-11.8 Services in an Expeditionary Environment

MISCELLANEOUS:

ADMINISTRATIVE INSTRUCTIONS: Appropriated Funds should be used as the primary source for supplies and equipment.

4130-MGMT-2401: Monitor MCCS Hazardous Materials (HAZMAT) Merchandise

EVALUATION-CODED: NO   SUSTAINMENT INTERVAL: 12 months

GRADES: WO-1, CWO-2, CWO-3, CWO-4, CWO-5

INITIAL TRAINING SETTING: MOJT

CONDITION: Given a requirement.

STANDARD: Ensuring that all is stored, displayed, sold, and disposed of safely.

PERFORMANCE STEPS:
1. Ensure segregation of MCCS Hazardous products.
2. Maintain Material Safety Data Sheets.

REFERENCES:
1. 29 CFR 1910.120 Occupational Safety and Health Standards - Hazardous waste operations and emergency response
2. MCO P4790.2_ MIMMS Field Procedures Manual

4130-MGMT-2402: Evaluate a merchandise presentation

EVALUATION-CODED: NO   SUSTAINMENT INTERVAL: 12 months

GRADES: WO-1, CWO-2, CWO-3, CWO-4, CWO-5

INITIAL TRAINING SETTING: MOJT

CONDITION: Given the standards.

STANDARD: Ensuring corrective actions are completed.

PERFORMANCE STEPS:
1. Inspect the facility.
2. Direct corrective actions as needed.

REFERENCES:
1. MCO P1700.27B Marine Corps Community Services Policy Manual
2. MCO P1700.30 Marine Corps Community Services Business Operations Manual

---

4130-OPS-2501: Review customer satisfaction programs

EVALUATION-CODED: NO   **SUSTAINMENT INTERVAL:** 12 months

GRADES: WO-1, CWO-2, CWO-3, CWO-4, CWO-5

INITIAL TRAINING SETTING: MOJT

CONDITION: Given reports.

STANDARD: Ensuring MCCS compliance with standards of excellence.

PERFORMANCE STEPS:
1. Track follow on correspondence.
2. Review results.
3. Ensure corrective action is taken.

REFERENCES:
1. MCO P1700.30 Marine Corps Community Services Business Operations Manual

MISCELLANEOUS:

   ADMINISTRATIVE INSTRUCTIONS: The primary means of evaluating customer feedback are MCX Mystery Shops, Associate Satisfaction Index/Customer Satisfaction Index ASI/CSI and Interactive Customer Evaluation (ICE) forms. These tools are used to highlight best business practices or determine training opportunities.

4130-OPS-2502: Monitor special events

EVALUATION-CODED: NO   **SUSTAINMENT INTERVAL:** 12 months

GRADES: WO-1, CWO-2, CWO-3, CWO-4, CWO-5

INITIAL TRAINING SETTING: MOJT

CONDITION: Given a requirement.

STANDARD: Ensuring the event meets the goals and objectives.

PERFORMANCE STEPS:
1. Determine type of special event.
2. Obtain contracts.

3. Identify support and marketing requirements.
4. Schedule confirmation briefs.

REFERENCES:
1. MCO P1700.27B Marine Corps Community Services Policy Manual
2. MCO P1700.30 Marine Corps Community Services Business Operations Manual

---

4130-OPS-2503: Evaluate a marketing action plan

EVALUATION-CODED: NO   **SUSTAINMENT INTERVAL:** 12 months

GRADES: WO-1, CWO-2, CWO-3, CWO-4, CWO-5

INITIAL TRAINING SETTING: MOJT

CONDITION: Given a requirement.

STANDARD: Ensuring the plan promotes MCCS products, programs and services.

PERFORMANCE STEPS:
1. Review the plan.
2. Monitor the performance.
3. Provide feedback.

REFERENCES:
1. MCO P1700.27B Marine Corps Community Services Policy Manual
2. MCO P1700.30 Marine Corps Community Services Business Operations Manual

---

4130-OPS-2504: Analyze asset protection program

EVALUATION-CODED: NO   **SUSTAINMENT INTERVAL:** 12 months

GRADES: WO-1, CWO-2, CWO-3, CWO-4, CWO-5

INITIAL TRAINING SETTING: MOJT

CONDITION: Given a requirement.

STANDARD: Ensuring compliance in accordance MCO 4066.17.

PERFORMANCE STEPS:
1. Review safety and security procedures.
2. Assess internal control procedures.
3. Determine corrective action.

REFERENCES:
1. MCO 5100.8 Marine Corps Occupational Safety and Health (OSH) Policy Order (May 06)
2. MCO P1700.27B Marine Corps Community Services Policy Manual

3. MCO P1700.30 Marine Corps Community Services Business Operations Manual
4. MCO P4066.17 Marine Corps Exchange Security and Loss Prevention Manual
    (May 82)

4130-OPS-2505: Monitor inventories

EVALUATION-CODED: NO   **SUSTAINMENT INTERVAL**: 12 months

GRADES: WO-1, CWO-2, CWO-3, CWO-4, CWO-5

INITIAL TRAINING SETTING: MOJT

CONDITION: Given the requirement.

STANDARD: Ensuring 100% accountability.

PERFORMANCE STEPS:
1. Identify type of inventory.
2. Review the referenced publications.
3. Verify accuracy.
4. Review adjustments.
5. Report findings.

REFERENCES:
1. MCO P1700.27B Marine Corps Community Services Policy Manual
2. MCO P1700.30 Marine Corps Community Services Business Operations Manual
3. MCO P4066.17 Marine Corps Exchange Security and Loss Prevention Manual
    (May 82)

4130-OPS-2506: Review MCCS Safety/Health/Environmental Program

EVALUATION-CODED: NO   **SUSTAINMENT INTERVAL**: 12 months

GRADES: WO-1, CWO-2, CWO-3, CWO-4, CWO-5

INITIAL TRAINING SETTING: FORMAL

CONDITION: Given a requirement.

STANDARD: Ensuring facilities and staff are operating in accordance with MCO 5100.8.

PERFORMANCE STEPS:
1. Inspect areas.
2. Review checklist.
3. Ensure safety representatives are assigned.
4. Ensure correction of deficiencies.

REFERENCES:
1. MCO 5100.29_ Marine Corps Safety Program

2. MCO 5100.8 Marine Corps Occupational Safety and Health (OSH) Policy Order (May 06)
3. MCO P1700.27B Marine Corps Community Services Policy Manual
4. MCO P1700.30 Marine Corps Community Services Business Operations Manual

---

4130-OPS-2507: Monitor food and beverage operations

EVALUATION-CODED: NO   **SUSTAINMENT INTERVAL:** 12 months

INITIAL TRAINING SETTING: FORMAL

CONDITION: Given a facility.

STANDARD: Ensuring the financial goals and objectives are attained in accordance with MCO 1700.30.

PERFORMANCE STEPS:
1. Review procedures of operation.
2. Analyze financial statement.
3. Review menus.
4. Audit sale price based on cost of goods.
5. Verify monthly inventory.
6. Ensure implementation of Controlling Alcohol Responsibility & Effectively (C.A.R.E.) program.

REFERENCES:
1. MCO 1700.22 Alcohol Beverage Control in the Marine Corps
2. MCO P1700.27B Marine Corps Community Services Policy Manual
3. MCO P1700.30 Marine Corps Community Services Business Operations Manual
4. MCO P7010.20 Marine Corps Community Services Nonappropriated Fund Procurement Policy
5. NAVMED P-5010 Navy Sanitation

4130-OPS-2508: Review SERVSAFE program

EVALUATION-CODED: NO   **SUSTAINMENT INTERVAL:** 12 months

GRADES: WO-1, CWO-2, CWO-3, CWO-4, CWO-5

INITIAL TRAINING SETTING: FORMAL

CONDITION: Given a MCCS food service operation.

STANDARD: Ensuring employees are certified and adhering to the program.

PERFORMANCE STEPS:
1. Ensure compliance.
2. Review employee training files.

REFERENCES:
1. MCO P1700.27B Marine Corps Community Services Policy Manual
2. MCO P1700.30 Marine Corps Community Services Business Operations Manual

MCCS T&R MANUAL

CHAPTER 5

MOS 4133 INDIVIDUAL EVENTS

MCCS T&R MANUAL

CHAPTER 5

MOS 4133 INDIVIDUAL EVENTS

5000. PURPOSE. This chapter contains individual training events for the Marine Corps Community Services Marine.

5001. EVENT CODING. Events in the T&R Manual are depicted with an up to 12 field alphanumeric system, i.e. XXXX-XXXX-XXXX. This chapter utilizes the following methodology:

a. Field one. Each event starts with 4133, indicating that the event is for MOS 4133, Marine Corps Community Services Marine.

b. Field two. This field is alpha characters indicating a functional area. In this chapter, the functional areas are as follows:

Code	Description	Example
CONT	Contracting/Contracting Services	4130-CONT-XXXX
EXPD	Expeditionary Operations	4130-EXPD-XXXX
FMGT	Financial Management	4130-FMGT-XXXX
MGMT	Basic Management	4130-MGMT-XXXX
OPS	Business Operations	4130-OPS-XXXX

c. Field three. All individual events within T&R Manuals are either 1000-level for events taught at MOS-producing formal schools or 2000-level for events taught at advanced-level schools or MOJT. This chapter contains 2000-level events only.

5002. INITIAL TRAINING SETTING. The tasks marked "Formal School" in this manual refer to Civilian establishments. The Marine Corps Community Services MOS does not currently have military training schools. Officer and Enlisted personnel must attend civilian establishments to attain the qualifications and certifications they require to perform certain duties. A list of required and recommended training is provided in Appendix A.

5003. INDEX OF INDIVIDUAL EVENTS

Event Code	Event	Page
	2000-LEVEL	
4133-CONT-2101	Monitor performance of MCCS contracts	5-4
4133-CONT-2102	Monitor concessionaire program	5-4
4133-CONT-2103	Conduct contracting/procurement	5-5
4133-EXPD-2201	Prepare MCCS assets for embarkation	5-6
4133-EXPD-2202	Establish MCCS field facilities	5-6
4133-EXPD-2203	Operate MCCS facilities	5-7
4133-EXPD-2204	Coordinate recreational activities and special events	5-8
4133-EXPD-2205	Execute a preventative maintenance plan	5-9
4133-EXPD-2206	Conduct Warrior Express Service Team "WES-T"	5-9
4133-EXPD-2207	Conduct patron survey	5-10
4133-EXPD-2208	Retrograde MCCS field facilities	5-10
4133-FMGT-2301	Analyze a financial statement (cost center level)	5-11
4133-FMGT-2302	Prepare a budget (cost center level)	5-12
4133-FMGT-2303	Approve payroll	5-12
4133-FMGT-2304	Maintain change fund accountability	5-13
4133-FMGT-2305	Complete daily activity reports	5-13
4133-FMGT-2306	Maintain official records	5-14
4133-FMGT-2307	Request APF fund support	5-14
4133-MGMT-2401	Conduct daily inspection of MCCS activity	5-15
4133-MGMT-2402	Manage MCCS Hazardous Materials Merchandise	5-15
4133-MGMT-2403	Manage MCCS Asset Protection Program	5-16
4133-MGMT-2404	Manage visual merchandise presentations	5-16
4133-MGMT-2405	Prepare inventory adjustment	5-17
4133-MGMT-2406	Survey merchandise	5-17
4133-OPS-2501	Execute visual merchandising plan	5-18
4133-OPS-2502	Supervise receiving procedures	5-18
4133-OPS-2503	Conduct transfer of goods	5-18
4133-OPS-2504	Manage warehouse operations	5-19
4133-OPS-2505	Supervise Mystery Shop Program and customer comments	5-19
4133-OPS-2506	Conduct inventory (property and equipment)	5-20
4133-OPS-2507	Prepare for inventory (retail)	5-20
4133-OPS-2508	Conduct retail inventory	5-21
4133-OPS-2509	Supervise sales procedures	5-21
4133-OPS-2510	Manage food and beverage operations	5-22
4133-OPS-2511	Provide support for entertainment	5-23
4133-OPS-2512	Organize special events	5-23
4133-OPS-2513	Monitor gaming devices	5-24
4133-OPS-2514	Operate firearm cost center	5-24

5004. 2000-LEVEL EVENTS

<u>4133-CONT-2101</u>: Monitor performance of MCCS contracts

<u>EVALUATION-CODED</u>: NO   <u>SUSTAINMENT INTERVAL</u>: 12 months

<u>GRADES</u>: GYSGT, MSGT, MGYSGT

<u>INITIAL TRAINING SETTING</u>: FORMAL

<u>CONDITION</u>: Given the contract requirements and references.

<u>STANDARD</u>: Ensuring all contractual obligations and regulations are IAW MCO P7010.20.

<u>PERFORMANCE STEPS</u>:
1. Review contract.
2. Conduct inspection schedule (monthly, quarterly, random).
3. Verify payment invoices.
4. Report non-compliance to the Contracting Officer.

<u>REFERENCES</u>:
1. DOD 5500.7-R Joint Ethics Regulation (JER)
2. DODI 1015.10 Programs for Military Morale, Welfare, and Recreation (MWR)
3. DODI 4105.71 Nonappropriated Fund (NAF) Procurement
4. DoDD 1015.2 Military Morale, Welfare and Recreation
5. DoDD 4105.67 Nonappropriated Fund (NAF) Procurement Policy
6. JP 1-0 Personnel Support to Joint Operations
7. MCO P1700.27B Marine Corps Community Services Policy Manual
8. MCO P1700.29 Marine Corps Semper Fit Program Manual
9. MCO P1700.30 Marine Corps Community Services Business Operations Manual
10. MCO P7010.20 Marine Corps Community Services Nonappropriated Fund Procurement Policy

---

<u>4133-CONT-2102</u>: Establish concessionaire program

<u>EVALUATION-CODED</u>: NO   <u>SUSTAINMENT INTERVAL</u>: 12 months

<u>GRADES</u>: GYSGT, MSGT, MGYSGT

<u>INITIAL TRAINING SETTING</u>: FORMAL

<u>CONDITION</u>: Given applications from concessionaires, adequate space for type of concession requested, and references.

<u>STANDARD</u>: Ensuring patrons' needs are met and operating in accordance with MCO 1700.30.

<u>PERFORMANCE STEPS</u>:
1. Determine concession needs based on patron desires.
2. Award the contract

3. Execute control measures to ensure only authorized items are sold.
4. Conduct audits.

REFERENCES:
1. DODI 1015.10 Programs for Military Morale, Welfare, and Recreation (MWR)
2. DODI 4105.71 Nonappropriated Fund (NAF) Procurement
3. DoDD 1015.2 Military Morale, Welfare and Recreation
4. DoDD 4105.67 Nonappropriated Fund (NAF) Procurement Policy
5. JP 1-0 Personnel Support to Joint Operations
6. MCO P1700.27B Marine Corps Community Services Policy Manual
7. MCO P1700.29 Marine Corps Semper Fit Program Manual
8. MCO P1700.30 Marine Corps Community Services Business Operations Manual
9. MCO P7010.20 Marine Corps Community Services Nonappropriated Fund Procurement Policy

MISCELLANEOUS:

ADMINISTRATIVE INSTRUCTIONS: SGT & SSGT at the following commands may be required to monitor concessionaires: Garden City, NY, Bridgeport, CA, Barstow, CA.

4133-CONT-2103: Conduct contracting/procument

EVALUATION-CODED: NO   **SUSTAINMENT INTERVAL:** 12 months

GRADES: GYSGT, MSGT, MGYSGT

INITIAL TRAINING SETTING: FORMAL

CONDITION: Given a requirement.

STANDARD: Ensuring requested goods and services are purchased in accordance with MCO P7010.20.

PERFORMANCE STEPS:
1. Determine purchasing requirements.
2. Ensure proper funding (Non-Appropriated Funds or Appropriated Funds).
3. Contract for goods and services.
4. Ensure contract compliance.

REFERENCES:
1. DODI 1015.10 Programs for Military Morale, Welfare, and Recreation (MWR)
2. DODI 4105.71 Nonappropriated Fund (NAF) Procurement
3. DoDD 1015.2 Military Morale, Welfare and Recreation
4. DoDD 4105.67 Nonappropriated Fund (NAF) Procurement Policy
5. JP 1-0 Personnel Support to Joint Operations
6. MCO P1700.27B Marine Corps Community Services Policy Manual
7. MCO P1700.29 Marine Corps Semper Fit Program Manual
8. MCO P1700.30 Marine Corps Community Services Business Operations Manual
9. MCO P7010.20 Marine Corps Community Services Nonappropriated Fund Procurement Policy

---

4133-EXPD-2201: Prepare MCCS assets for embarkation

EVALUATION-CODED: NO   **SUSTAINMENT INTERVAL**: 12 months

GRADES: SGT, SSGT, GYSGT, MSGT, MGYSGT

INITIAL TRAINING SETTING: MOJT

CONDITION: Given a requirement.

STANDARD: Ensuring the Tactical Field Exchange merchandise and equipment is properly packed and secured for transport.

PERFORMANCE STEPS:
1. Review referenced publications.
2. Identify required documentation.
3. Coordinate internal/external support.
4. Inventory assets.
5. Identify hazardous materials.
6. Supervise loading.

REFERENCES:
1. 29 CFR 1910.120 Occupational Safety and Health Standards - Hazardous waste operations and emergency response
2. MCO P1700.27B Marine Corps Community Services Policy Manual
3. MCO P1700.30 Marine Corps Community Services Business Operations Manual
4. MCWP 4-11 Tactical-Level Logistics
5. MCWP 4_1 LOGISTICS OPERATIONS

SUPPORT REQUIREMENTS:

   EQUIPMENT: Coordinate heavy equipment support.

4133-EXPD-2202: Establish MCCS field facilities

EVALUATION-CODED: NO   **SUSTAINMENT INTERVAL**: 12 months

DESCRIPTION: An MCCS field facility may include retail, food and beverage, business recreation, communications, Semper Fit and morale centers.

GRADES: SGT, SSGT, GYSGT, MSGT, MGYSGT

INITIAL TRAINING SETTING: MOJT

CONDITION: In an expeditionary environment, given a requirement support and T/O&E equipment.

STANDARD: Ensuring that space, equipment and personnel requirements are adequate to meet the mission requirements.

PERFORMANCE STEPS:
1. Determine number of personnel to be supported.
2. Verify duration of operation.

3. Identify number of personnel for staffing.
4. Establish assortment.
5. Determine source of supply.
6. Determine logistical support requirements.
7. Obtain internal operational supplies/equipment.
8. Train/orientate personnel as required.
9. Request appropriate structures.
10. Conduct inventory before operation.
11. Evaluate operation for effectiveness and possible revisions.

REFERENCES:
1. DODI 1015.10 Programs for Military Morale, Welfare, and Recreation (MWR)
2. DoDD 1015.2 Military Morale, Welfare and Recreation
3. JP 1-0 Personnel Support to Joint Operations
4. MCO P1700.27B Marine Corps Community Services Policy Manual
5. MCO P1700.29 Marine Corps Semper Fit Program Manual
6. MCO P1700.30 Marine Corps Community Services Business Operations Manual
7. MCWP 4-11.8 Services in an Expeditionary Environment

SUPPORT REQUIREMENTS:

ROOMS/BUILDINGS: Determine space requirements prior to implementation of facility. Acquire necessary space for required recreation needs. Size of space needed will be determined by the needs assessment and the space available.

EQUIPMENT: Equipment will be determined during the needs assessment.

UNITS/PERSONNEL: The following personnel are required to assist the MCCS personnel in transporting and the start-up and tear-down of the Tactical Field Exchange. This list of personnel includes, but is not limited to the following: Electrician (MOS 1141); Electrical Repair Specialist (MOS 1171); Engineer Equipment Operator (MOS 1145); and Motor Vehicle Operator (MOS 3531).

4133-EXPD-2203: Operate MCCS facilities

EVALUATION-CODED: NO   **SUSTAINMENT INTERVAL:** 12 months

GRADES: SSGT, GYSGT, MSGT, MGYSGT

INITIAL TRAINING SETTING: MOJT

CONDITION: In an Expeditionary environment, given publications, Table of Organization and Equipment (TO/E), directives, personnel, administrative equipment and references.

STANDARD: Ensuring operating, administration, and accounting procedures are performed daily in accordance with Standard Operating Procedures (SOP).

PERFORMANCE STEPS:
1. Identify type of facility.
2. Assign personnel to perform task identified.

3. Establish desktop procedures.
4. Maintain turnover file procedures.
5. Maintain records as required.
6. Adhere to accounting procedures.
7. Maintain asset protections/loss prevention procedures.
8. Maintain accountability of inventory.

REFERENCES:
1. MCO P1700.30 Marine Corps Community Services Business Operations Manual
2. MCO P4066.17 Marine Corps Exchange Security and Loss Prevention Manual (May 82)
3. MCWP 4-1 Logistics Operations
4. MCWP 4-11 Tactical-Level Logistics
5. MCWP 4-11.8 Services in an Expeditionary Environment
6. MCWP 4-12 Operational-Level Logistics

MISCELLANEOUS:

ADMINISTRATIVE INSTRUCTIONS: When dealing with contracted labor, ensure compliance of applicable position descriptions.

4133-EXPD-2204: Coordinate recreational activities and special events

EVALUATION-CODED: NO   **SUSTAINMENT INTERVAL:** 12 months

GRADES: SGT, SSGT, GYSGT, MSGT, MGYSGT

INITIAL TRAINING SETTING: MOJT

CONDITION: Given regulations and a requirement.

STANDARD: Providing an opportunity for patrons to participate in quality of life programs.

PERFORMANCE STEPS:
1. Assess customer's interests.
2. Identify financial requirements.
3. Plan recurring and / non-recurring activities based on facility hours, Command mission and population.
4. Identify resources (equipment, staff/volunteers, and supplies).
5. Evaluate activities.
6. Develop after action report.

REFERENCES:
1. DODI 1015.10 Programs for Military Morale, Welfare, and Recreation (MWR)
2. JP 1-0 Personnel Support to Joint Operations
3. MCO P1700.27B Marine Corps Community Services Policy Manual
4. MCO P1700.29 Marine Corps Semper Fit Program Manual
5. MCO P1700.30 Marine Corps Community Services Business Operations Manual

MISCELLANEOUS:

ADMINISTRATIVE INSTRUCTIONS: Special events must be coordinated with local Commands to ensure policies and regulations are followed.

4133-EXPD-2205: Execute a preventative maintenance plan

EVALUATION-CODED: NO   SUSTAINMENT INTERVAL: 12 months

GRADES: SGT, SSGT, GYSGT

INITIAL TRAINING SETTING: MOJT

CONDITION: Given MCCS equipment, regulations, references and a requirement.

STANDARD: Maximizing equipment lifecycle.

PERFORMANCE STEPS:
1. Identify maintenance requirements.
2. Develop an inspection schedule.
3. Identify broken and/or unserviceable equipment.
4. Repair/replace equipment as required.

REFERENCES:
1. JP 1-0 Personnel Support to Joint Operations
2. MCO P1700.27B Marine Corps Community Services Policy Manual
3. MCO P1700.29 Marine Corps Semper Fit Program Manual

MISCELLANEOUS:

ADMINISTRATIVE INSTRUCTIONS: MCCS equipment includes but is not limited to: registers, computers, laptops and exercise equipment.

4133-EXPD-2206: Conduct Warrior Express Service Team "WES-T"

EVALUATION-CODED: NO   SUSTAINMENT INTERVAL: 12 months

GRADES: SGT, SSGT, GYSGT

INITIAL TRAINING SETTING: MOJT

CONDITION: Giving the requirement.

STANDARD: Enhancing the quality of life of forward deployed personnel.

PERFORMANCE STEPS:
1. Coordinate all external support.
2. Identify personnel.
3. Prepare internal assets.
4. Asset oversight.

5. Perform operations.
6. Conduct retro grade.

REFERENCES:
1. MCO P1700.27B Marine Corps Community Services Policy Manual
2. MCO P1700.30 Marine Corps Community Services Business Operations Manual

---

4133-EXPD-2207: Conduct patron survey

EVALUATION-CODED: NO   **SUSTAINMENT INTERVAL:** 12 months

GRADES: SGT, SSGT, GYSGT

INITIAL TRAINING SETTING: MOJT

CONDITION: Given MCCS operations and customer base.

STANDARD: Identifying deficiencies and make operational changes.

PERFORMANCE STEPS:
1. Administer survey
2. Submit survey results.
3. Make operational changes.

REFERENCES:
1. DODI 1015.10 Programs for Military Morale, Welfare, and Recreation (MWR)
2. DODI 1015.14 Establishment, Management, and Control of Nonappropriated Fund Instrumentalities and Financial Management of Supporting Resources
3. DODI 4105.71 Nonappropriated Fund (NAF) Procurement
4. DoDD 1015.2 Military Morale, Welfare and Recreation
5. DoDD 4105.67 Nonappropriated Fund (NAF) Procurement Policy
6. JP 1-0 Personnel Support to Joint Operations
7. MCO P1700.27B Marine Corps Community Services Policy Manual
8. MCO P1700.29 Marine Corps Semper Fit Program Manual
9. MCO P1700.30 Marine Corps Community Services Business Operations Manual
10. MCO P7010.20 Marine Corps Community Services Nonappropriated Fund Procurement Policy

---

4133-EXPD-2208: Retrograde MCCS Field Facilities

EVALUATION-CODED: NO   **SUSTAINMENT INTERVAL:** 12 months

GRADES: SGT, SSGT, GYSGT

INITIAL TRAINING SETTING: MOJT

CONDITION: When activities are no longer required.

STANDARD: Ensuring all assets are properly accounted for.

PERFORMANCE STEPS:
1. Conduct inventory.
2. Safeguard assets.
3. Secure all negotiable instruments.
4. Package merchandise, supplies, and equipment.
5. Arrange logistical support for embarkation.
6. Seal containers.
7. Track containers.

REFERENCES:
1. DODI 1015.10 Programs for Military Morale, Welfare, and Recreation (MWR)
2. DoDD 1015.2 Military Morale, Welfare and Recreation
3. JP 1-0 Personnel Support to Joint Operations
4. MCO P1700.27B Marine Corps Community Services Policy Manual
5. MCO P1700.29 Marine Corps Semper Fit Program Manual
6. MCO P1700.30 Marine Corps Community Services Business Operations Manual
7. MCWP 4-1 Logistics Operations
8. MCWP 4-11 Tactical-Level Logistics

SUPPORT REQUIREMENTS:

UNITS/PERSONNEL: The following personnel are required to assist the MCCS personnel in transporting and the start-up and tear-down of the Tactical Field Exchange. This list of personnel includes, but is not limited to the following: Electrician (MOS 1141); Electrical Repair Specialist (MOS 1171); Engineer Equipment Operator (MOS 1145); and Motor Vehicle Operator (MOS 3531).

4133-FMGT-2301: Analyze a financial statement (cost center level)

EVALUATION-CODED: NO   **SUSTAINMENT INTERVAL:** 12 months

DESCRIPTION: Overall business operations.

GRADES: SGT, SSGT, GYSGT, MSGT, MGYSGT

INITIAL TRAINING SETTING: FORMAL

CONDITION: Given profit, loss statements, budget and variance reports.

STANDARD: Measuring profitability and performance IAW MCO 1700.30.

PERFORMANCE STEPS:
1. Review monthly performance.
2. Determine if goals are met.
3. Recommend corrective actions.

REFERENCES:
1. DODI 1015.10 Programs for Military Morale, Welfare, and Recreation (MWR)
2. DODI 1015.14 Establishment, Management, and Control of Nonappropriated Fund Instrumentalities and Financial Management of Supporting Resources
3. DoDD 1015.2 Military Morale, Welfare and Recreation

4. MCO P1700.27B Marine Corps Community Services Policy Manual
5. MCO P1700.30 Marine Corps Community Services Business Operations Manual

---

4133-FMGT-2302: Prepare a budget (cost center level)

EVALUATION-CODED: NO   **SUSTAINMENT INTERVAL:** 12 months

GRADES: SGT, SSGT, GYSGT, MSGT, MGYSGT

INITIAL TRAINING SETTING: FORMAL

CONDITION: Given historical information, trend analysis and, operational tempo.

STANDARD: Defining the financial goals and objectives.

PERFORMANCE STEPS:
1. Review current year performance.
2. Calculate specific budget requirement.
3. Forecast sales.
4. Forecast fixed and variable expenses.
5. Ensure goals and objectives are calculated.

REFERENCES:
1. DODI 1015.10 Programs for Military Morale, Welfare, and Recreation (MWR)
2. DODI 1015.14 Establishment, Management, and Control of Nonappropriated Fund Instrumentalities and Financial Management of Supporting Resources
3. DoDD 1015.2 Military Morale, Welfare and Recreation
4. MCO P1700.27B Marine Corps Community Services Policy Manual
5. MCO P1700.30 Marine Corps Community Services Business Operations Manual

---

4133-FMGT-2303: Approve payroll

EVALUATION-CODED: NO   **SUSTAINMENT INTERVAL:** 12 months

GRADES: SGT, SSGT, GYSGT, MSGT, MGYSGT

INITIAL TRAINING SETTING: FORMAL

CONDITION: Given assigned schedules, hours worked and payroll management system.

STANDARD: Ensuring the accuracy of employee hours worked is validated.

PERFORMANCE STEPS:
1. Follow time-keeping procedures.
2. Verify payroll reporting.

REFERENCES:
1. MCO P1700.27B Marine Corps Community Services Policy Manual
2. MCO P5300.9 Marine Corps Nonappropriated Funds Instrumentalities Personnel Manual

---

4133-FMGT-2304: Maintain change fund accountability

EVALUATION-CODED: NO   **SUSTAINMENT INTERVAL:** 12 months

DESCRIPTION: Maintaining cash custody procedures is defined as managing operation change fund.

GRADES: SGT, SSGT, GYSGT, MSGT, MGYSGT

INITIAL TRAINING SETTING: FORMAL

CONDITION: Given a requirement.

STANDARD: Ensuring all cash custody procedures are followed.

PERFORMANCE STEPS:
1. Sign for funds.
2. Issue funds.
3. Submit deposits in accordance with local policy.
4. Conduct random safe and register counts/audits.

REFERENCES:
1. DoD 7000.14-R DoD Financial Management Regulation (DoDFMR), Volume 7A
2. MCO P1700.27B Marine Corps Community Services Policy Manual
3. MCO P1700.30 Marine Corps Community Services Business Operations Manual
4. MCO P4066.17 Marine Corps Exchange Security and Loss Prevention Manual (May 82)
5. MCWP 4-11.8 Services in an Expeditionary Environment

4133-FMGT-2305: Complete daily activity reports

EVALUATION-CODED: NO   **SUSTAINMENT INTERVAL:** 12 months

GRADES: SGT, SSGT, GYSGT

INITIAL TRAINING SETTING: MOJT

CONDITION: Given a requirement.

STANDARD: Ensuring the form is completed and submitted for each day.

PERFORMANCE STEPS:
1. Compile all daily paper work for the business day.
2. Total all reports.
3. Submit each report with MCCS accounting daily.
4. Validate each report.

REFERENCES:
1. MCO P1700.27B Marine Corps Community Services Policy Manual

MISCELLANEOUS:

ADMINISTRATIVE INSTRUCTIONS: For retail inspections use the "From their Eyes" Checklist.

4133-FMGT-2306: Maintain official records

EVALUATION-CODED: NO   **SUSTAINMENT INTERVAL:** 12 months

GRADES: SGT, SSGT, GYSGT, MSGT, MGYSGT

INITIAL TRAINING SETTING: MOJT

CONDITION: Given the requirement.

STANDARD: Ensuring all required data is retained as directed.

PERFORMANCE STEPS:
1. Receive files from various sources.
2. Sort files.
3. File according to different categories.
4. Secure records in accordance with procedures.

REFERENCES:
1. MCO P1700.27B Marine Corps Community Services Policy Manual
2. MCO P5300.9 Marine Corps Nonappropriated Funds Instrumentalities Personnel Manual
3. SECNAVINST P5212.5 Disposal Navy/Marine Corps Records

4133-FMGT-2307: Request APF fund support

EVALUATION-CODED: NO   **SUSTAINMENT INTERVAL:** 12 months

GRADES: GYSGT, MSGT, MGYSGT

INITIAL TRAINING SETTING: FORMAL

CONDITION: In a MCCS Food and Hospitality environment given Profit and Loss statement, Budget, variance analysis, historical data and other supporting financial data and an established need.

STANDARD: To ensure food and hospitality facilities are appropriately reimbursed for supporting official command functions.

PERFORMANCE STEPS:
1. Gather financial data.
2. Gather historical data.
3. Submit the appropriate documentation/request.

REFERENCES:
1. DoD 7000.14-R DoD Financial Management Regulation (DoDFMR), Volume 7A
2. MCO P1700.27B Marine Corps Community Services Policy Manual
3. MCO P4066.17 Marine Corps Exchange Security and Loss Prevention Manual (May 82)
4. MCWP 4-11.8 Services in an Expeditionary Environment

4133-MGMT-2401: Conduct daily inspection of MCCS activity

EVALUATION-CODED: NO   **SUSTAINMENT INTERVAL:** 12 months

GRADES: SGT, SSGT, GYSGT

INITIAL TRAINING SETTING: MOJT

CONDITION: In a MCCS activity, given publications, an evaluation checklist, and references.

STANDARD: Ensuring facilities are clean, safe and operational.

PERFORMANCE STEPS:
1. Utilize checklist.
2. Correct discrepancies.

REFERENCES:
1. MCO P1700.27B Marine Corps Community Services Policy Manual
2. MCO P1700.30 Marine Corps Community Services Business Operations Manual
3. MCO P4066.17 Marine Corps Exchange Security and Loss Prevention Manual (May 82)

4133-MGMT-2402: Manage MCCS Hazardous Materials Merchandise

EVALUATION-CODED: NO   **SUSTAINMENT INTERVAL:** 12 months

GRADES: SGT, SSGT, GYSGT

INITIAL TRAINING SETTING: MOJT

CONDITION: Given applicable technical manuals and directives.

STANDARD: Ensuring that all HAZMAT merchandise is stored, displayed, sold, and disposed of safely if surveyed.

PERFORMANCE STEPS:
1. Implement Plan O- Gram.
2. Maintain Material Safety Data Sheets.
3. Ensure segregation of MCCS Hazardous products from consumables.

REFERENCES:
1. 29 CFR 1910.120 Occupational Safety and Health Standards - Hazardous waste operations and emergency response
2. MCO P4790.2_ MIMMS Field Procedures Manual

4133-MGMT-2403: Manage MCCS Asset Protection Program

EVALUATION-CODED: NO   **SUSTAINMENT INTERVAL:** 12 months

GRADES: SGT, SSGT, GYSGT, MSGT, MGYSGT

INITIAL TRAINING SETTING: MOJT

CONDITION: Given a requirement.

STANDARD: Mitigating loss and damages to MCCS assets.

PERFORMANCE STEPS:
1. Adhere to SOP for safety and security.
2. Monitor internal control procedures.
3. Assign personnel responsible for safety and security.
4. Ensure the security program involves coordination with the Provost Marshal and other law enforcement agencies.
5. Ensure correction of deficiencies.
6. Complete daily safety and security checklist.
7. Validate key logs daily.
8. Ensure safe combinations and exterior door locks are changed as required.
9. In MCX facilities, monitor exception reporting and track variance reports.

REFERENCES:
1. MCO 5100.8 Marine Corps Occupational Safety and Health (OSH) Policy Order (May 06)
2. MCO P1700.27B Marine Corps Community Services Policy Manual
3. MCO P4066.17 Marine Corps Exchange Security and Loss Prevention Manual (May 82)

4133-MGMT-2404: Manage visual merchandise presentations

EVALUATION-CODED: NO   **SUSTAINMENT INTERVAL:** 12 months

GRADES: SGT, SSGT, GYSGT

INITIAL TRAINING SETTING: MOJT

CONDITION: Given retail selling space, merchandise, display equipment, visual props, Plan-O-Grams and staff.

STANDARD: Ensuring displays meet MCX store standards and follows directed Plan-O-Grams.

PERFORMANCE STEPS:
1. Utilize Plan O Grams and standard layout.
2. Ensure that the visual merchandiser coordinates with store management.
3. Ensure appropriate displays are created.

REFERENCES:
1. MCO P1700.27B Marine Corps Community Services Policy Manual

---

4133-MGMT-2405: Prepare inventory adjustment

EVALUATION-CODED: NO   **SUSTAINMENT INTERVAL:** 12 months

DESCRIPTION: Does not include merchandise surveys.

GRADES: GYSGT, MSGT, MGYSGT

INITIAL TRAINING SETTING: MOJT

CONDITION: Given a requirement.

STANDARD: Ensuring 100% accountability and accuracy.

PERFORMANCE STEPS:
1. Conduct research on how items were received.
2. Gather all inventory data.
3. Review inventory movement on items in question.
4. Identify discrepancies in receiving procedures.
5. Verify correct quantities.
6. Forward changes to appropriate MCCS representative for input.

REFERENCES:
1. MCO P1700.27B Marine Corps Community Services Policy Manual
2. MCO P4066.17 Marine Corps Exchange Security and Loss Prevention Manual (May 82)

4133-MGMT-2406: Survey merchandise

EVALUATION-CODED: NO   **SUSTAINMENT INTERVAL:** 12 months

GRADES: SGT, SSGT, GYSGT

INITIAL TRAINING SETTING: MOJT

CONDITION: Given a requirement.

STANDARD: Ensuring 100% accountability.

PERFORMANCE STEPS:
1. Segregate damaged/dated goods.
2. Complete inventory adjustment form.
3. Coordinate Asset Protection.

4. Destroy merchandise.
5. Forward documentation.

REFERENCES:
1. MCO P1700.27B Marine Corps Community Services Policy Manual
2. MCO P4066.17 Marine Corps Exchange Security and Loss Prevention Manual
    (May 82)

4133-OPS-2501: Execute visual merchandising plan

EVALUATION-CODED: NO   SUSTAINMENT INTERVAL: 12 months

GRADES: SGT, SSGT, GYSGT, MSGT, MGYSGT

INITIAL TRAINING SETTING: FORMAL

CONDITION: In a MCCS facility, given merchandise, store layout, display, display equipment, visual props, staff, and the references.

STANDARD: To ensure that visual merchandising reflects the character of the store, sets the mood, highlights new items, and encourages the purchase of the items displayed.

PERFORMANCE STEPS:
1. Ensure all visual merchandise staff coordinates with the merchandise staff.
2. Ensure proper displays are created.

REFERENCES:
1. MCO P1700.27B Marine Corps Community Services Policy Manual

---

4133-OPS-2502: Supervise receiving procedures

EVALUATION-CODED: NO   SUSTAINMENT INTERVAL: 12 months

GRADES: WO-1, CWO-2, CWO-3, CWO-4, CWO-5

INITIAL TRAINING SETTING: MOJT

CONDITION: In a Marine Corps Exchange facility.

STANDARD: Ensuring 100% accuracy to include timeliness of door to floor delivery using a retail management system.

PERFORMANCE STEPS:
1. Verify all merchandise is accounted for and matches the invoice.
2. Inspect goods for damaged or concealed shortages.
3. Verify all goods are properly ticketed when required.
4. Verify all overage/shortage.
5. Process Frustrated Freight.

REFERENCES:
1. MCO P1700.27B Marine Corps Community Services Policy Manual
2. MCO P1700.30 Marine Corps Community Services Business Operations Manual

---

4133-OPS-2503: Conduct transfer of goods

EVALUATION-CODED: NO   **SUSTAINMENT INTERVAL:** 12 months

INITIAL TRAINING SETTING: MOJT

CONDITION: Given the requirement.

STANDARD: Ensuring 100% accountability of merchandise.

PERFORMANCE STEPS:
1. Identify merchandise.
2. Determine who is authorized to receive goods.
3. Determine type of transfer.
4. Obtain receipt of goods.

REFERENCES:
1. MCO P1700.27B Marine Corps Community Services Policy Manual
2. MCO P1700.30 Marine Corps Community Services Business Operations Manual

---

4133-OPS-2504: Manage warehouse operations

EVALUATION-CODED: NO   **SUSTAINMENT INTERVAL:** 12 months

GRADES: SGT, SSGT, GYSGT

INITIAL TRAINING SETTING: MOJT

CONDITION: Given merchandise, equipment and personnel.

STANDARD: Receiving, storing and redistributing merchandise without loss or damage.

PERFORMANCE STEPS:
1. Verify accurate receipt of all equipment, merchandise and product.
2. Arrange stock in a "first in, first out" (FIFO) basis and separated it by type.
3. Verify security is maintained to prevent pilferage and damage.
4. Monitor issuing and transfer of goods.

REFERENCES:
1. MCO P1700.30 Marine Corps Community Services Business Operations Manual
2. MCO P4066.17 Marine Corps Exchange Security and Loss Prevention Manual (May 82)

4133-OPS-2505: Supervise Mystery Shop Program and customer comments

EVALUATION-CODED: NO   **SUSTAINMENT INTERVAL:** 12 months

GRADES: SGT, SSGT, GYSGT, MSGT, MGYSGT

INITIAL TRAINING SETTING: MOJT

CONDITION: Given reports.

STANDARD: Ensuring MCCS compliance with standards of excellence.

PERFORMANCE STEPS:
1. Solicit internal/external customer comments.
2. Reply to comments as required.
3. Review results
4. Take corrective action.
5. Reward excellence.
6. Publish periodic patron surveys.

REFERENCES:
1. MCO P1700.30 Marine Corps Community Services Business Operations Manual

MISCELLANEOUS:

   ADMINISTRATIVE INSTRUCTIONS: The primary means of evaluating customer feedback are MCX Mystery Shops, Associate Satisfaction Index/Customer Satisfaction Index ASI/CSI and Interactive Customer Evaluation (ICE) forms. These tools can be used to highlight best business practices or determine training opportunities.

4133-OPS-2506: Conduct inventory (property and equipment)

EVALUATION-CODED: NO   **SUSTAINMENT INTERVAL:** 12 months

GRADES: SGT, SSGT, GYSGT

INITIAL TRAINING SETTING: MOJT

CONDITION: Given a Consolidated Memorandum Receipt (CMR) and additional equipment.

STANDARD: Ensuring 100% accountability of MCCS property.

PERFORMANCE STEPS:
1. Conduct inventories as required by the references.
2. Verify NSN, property number and nomenclature.
3. Review and analyze results for accuracy.
4. Report discrepancies to applicable authorities.
5. Account for transfer of property.
6. Maintain records

REFERENCES:
1. MCO P11000.5 Real Property Facilities Manual, Vol IV
2. MCO P1700.27B Marine Corps Community Services Policy Manual

---

4133-OPS-2507: Prepare for inventory (retail)

EVALUATION-CODED: NO   SUSTAINMENT INTERVAL: 12 months

GRADES: SGT, SSGT, GYSGT

INITIAL TRAINING SETTING: MOJT

CONDITION: Given a MCX facility.

STANDARD: Ensuring that all lines of merchandise are ready for audit.

PERFORMANCE STEPS:
1. Review the referenced publications.
2. Confirm inventory dates.
3. Schedule employees.
4. Update floor plan.
5. Ensure fixture numbers are assigned to each fixture.

REFERENCES:
1. MCO P1700.27B Marine Corps Community Services Policy Manual
2. MCO P1700.30 Marine Corps Community Services Business Operations Manual
3. MCO P4066.17 Marine Corps Exchange Security and Loss Prevention Manual
    (May 82)

4133-OPS-2508: Conduct retail inventory

EVALUATION-CODED: NO   SUSTAINMENT INTERVAL: 12 months

GRADES: SGT, SSGT, GYSGT, MSGT, MGYSGT

INITIAL TRAINING SETTING: MOJT

CONDITION: In a MCCS facility, warehouse, or storage area, given floor plans, area tickets, inventory sheets, stock to be inventoried, and the references.

STANDARD: To ensure that all merchandise is inventoried.

PERFORMANCE STEPS:
1. Review the referenced publications.
2. Establish local policy where needed.
3. Establish inventory dates.
4. Ensure fixture numbers are assigned to each fixture.
5. Reconcile inventory variance reports
6. Evaluate procedures annually.

REFERENCES:
1. MCO P1700.27B Marine Corps Community Services Policy Manual

---

4133-OPS-2509:   Supervise sales procedures

EVALUATION-CODED: NO   SUSTAINMENT INTERVAL: 12 months

GRADES: SGT, SSGT, GYSGT, MSGT, MGYSGT

INITIAL TRAINING SETTING: FORMAL

CONDITION: In a MCCS activity, given cash registers, employees, RMS system, merchandise, and the references.

STANDARD: To ensure sales are properly captured in EPOS.

PERFORMANCE STEPS:
1. Verify all items are scanned and sold by Universal Product Code (retail).
2. Ensure cashiers are trained in the proper operation of all cash registers.
3. Verify appropriate personnel perform cash register readings/voids.
4. Ensure each cashier is provided separate change funds.
5. Account for credit card slips.
6. Enforce a tolerance (percentage or dollars) ratio of cash overage/shortage to sales total per cashier.
7. Identify end of shift overage/shortage per cashier and take appropriate action.
8. Review sales transactions to ensure there is no fraudulent activity.
9. Ensure refund procedures are followed.

REFERENCES:
1. MCO P1700.27B Marine Corps Community Services Policy Manual
2. MCO P4066.17 Marine Corps Exchange Security and Loss Prevention Manual (May 82)

4133-OPS-2510:   Manage food and beverage operations

EVALUATION-CODED: NO   SUSTAINMENT INTERVAL: 12 months

GRADES: SGT, SSGT, GYSGT

INITIAL TRAINING SETTING: FORMAL

CONDITION: In a Marine Corps Community Service environment, given a facility in a designated area.

STANDARD: Ensuring the MCCS food and beverage operation meets the standard cost of goods and labor with the goal of profitability.

PERFORMANCE STEPS:
1. Determine menu items.
2. Determine sale price based on cost of goods.

3. Establish PAR stocks.
4. Procure menu inventory.
5. Determine and procure equipment
6. Determine, obtain and train work force.
7. Establish procedures of operation and cost controls.
8. Establish health, safety, environmental and sanitation procedures.
9. Ensure implementation of Controlling Alcohol Responsibility & Effectively (C.A.R.E.) program.

REFERENCES:
1. MCO 1700.22 Alcohol Beverage Control in the Marine Corps
2. MCO P1700.27B Marine Corps Community Services Policy Manual
3. MCO P1700.30 Marine Corps Community Services Business Operations Manual
4. MCO P4200.15 Marine Corps Purchasing Procedures Manual - (obsolete MCO)

4133-OPS-2511: Provide support for entertainment

EVALUATION-CODED: NO   **SUSTAINMENT INTERVAL:** 12 months

DESCRIPTION: These entertainment venues are facilitated through the USO or Armed Forces Entertainment.

GRADES: SSGT, GYSGT, MSGT, MGYSGT

INITIAL TRAINING SETTING: MOJT

CONDITION: Given a location and the demand.

STANDARD: Ensuring the needs of the entertainer are provided and the event starts as scheduled.

PERFORMANCE STEPS:
1. Obtain contracts needed.
2. Identify entertainer needs.
3. Coordinate external support requirements.
4. Provide travel and life support.
5. Complete after action report.

REFERENCES:
1. MCO P1700.27B Marine Corps Community Services Policy Manual
2. MCO P1700.30 Marine Corps Community Services Business Operations Manual
3. MCO P4200.15 Marine Corps Purchasing Procedures Manual - (obsolete MCO)

4133-OPS-2512: Conduct Special Events

EVALUATION-CODED: NO   **SUSTAINMENT INTERVAL:** 12 months

GRADES: SSGT, GYSGT, MSGT, MGYSGT

INITIAL TRAINING SETTING: MOJT

CONDITION: Given a plan.

STANDARD: Ensuring the event meets the goals and objectives of the action officer.

PERFORMANCE STEPS:
1. Review the plan.
2. Review contracts.
3. Supervise or follow-up as required.
4. Complete after action report.

REFERENCES:
1. MCO P1700.27B Marine Corps Community Services Policy Manual
2. MCO P1700.30 Marine Corps Community Services Business Operations Manual

---

4133-OPS-2513: Monitor gaming devices

EVALUATION-CODED: NO   **SUSTAINMENT INTERVAL:** 12 months

DESCRIPTION: Gaming devices are only authorized in overseas commands.

GRADES: SGT, SSGT, GYSGT

INITIAL TRAINING SETTING: MOJT

CONDITION: Given an area designated for gaming operations and the references.

STANDARD: Ensuring the machines operate IAW MCO 1700.30, Chapter 11.

PERFORMANCE STEPS:
1. Maintain change fund.
2. Ensure machines are repaired in a timely manner.
3. Ensure only authorized persons play machines.
4. Inspect facilities regularly for asset protection.

REFERENCES:
1. MCO P1700.27B Marine Corps Community Services Policy Manual
2. MCO P1700.30 Marine Corps Community Services Business Operations Manual
3. MCO P4066.17 Marine Corps Exchange Security and Loss Prevention Manual (May 82)

4133-OPS-2514: Operate firearm cost center

EVALUATION-CODED: NO   **SUSTAINMENT INTERVAL:** 12 months

GRADES: SGT, SSGT, GYSGT

INITIAL TRAINING SETTING: MOJT

CONDITION: Given a MCX facility.

STANDARD: Maintaining the requirement for licensing in accordance with Alcohol, Tobacco and Firearms (ATF) guidelines.

PERFORMANCE STEPS:
1. Review the references.
2. Ensure administrative requirements are met.
3. Conduct receiving procedures.
4. Conduct transfers.
5. Enforce proper storage
6. Enforce display controls.
7. Process sales using required handling procedures.
8. Conduct inventory.

REFERENCES:
1. MCO P1700.30 Marine Corps Community Services Business Operations Manual
2. MCO P4066.17 Marine Corps Exchange Security and Loss Prevention Manual (May 82)

MCCS T&R MANUAL

APPENDIX A

MARINE CORPS COMMUNITY SERVICES COURSES/TRAINING

The following courses are a combination of training and professional development courses which are designed to provide developmental opportunities that will either certify Marines to execute their duties, or broaden their general knowledge. More information about the courses is available through the MCCS Training Catalog, Headquarters, United States Marine Corps, Personal & Family Readiness Division, 3044 Catlin Avenue, Quantico, VA 22134.

4100/SERGEANT
- 7 HABITS OF HIGHLY EFFECTIVE PEOPLE
- WORLD CLASS CUSTOMER SERVICE
- COMMUNICATION STRATEGIES THAT GET RESULTS
- RETAIL MATH 1
- CREATIVE TRAINING TECHNIQUES 1
- FORKLIFT CLASSES (MILITARY EBFL AND WAREHOUSE FORKLIFT)
- HUMVEE LICENSE (MILITARY)
- 7 TON LICENSE (MILITARY)
- SERVSAFE (F&H)
- SNACK BAR MANAGEMENT (F&H)
- TFE TRAINING
- PREVENTION OF SEXUAL HARASSMENT (POSH)
- ETHICS
- CONSTITUTION TRAINING

STAFF SERGEANT/GUNNERY SERGEANT
- LEADERSHIP SKILLS FOR MANAGERS
- APPLIED FINANCIAL PLANNING
- RETAIL MATH ADVANCED
- CREATIVE TRAINING TECHNIQUES II
- EMPLOYMENT LAW FOR MANAGERS
- MCCS MANAGERS COURSE
- RECREATION MANAGERS COURSE
- SOFTLINES MATERIALS
- HARDLINES/CONSUMABLES MATERIALS
- MARKETING MANAGERS COURSE
- CLUB MANAGEMENT SKILLS (F&H)
- ADVANCED CLUB MANAGEMENT SKILLS (F&H)
- FOOD AND BEVERAGE MANAGEMENT (F&H)

MASTER SERGEANT/MASTER GUNNERY SERGEANT
- EXECUTIVE SKILLS DEVELOPMENT
- MAKING MEETINGS WORK
- CONTRACTING COURSE BASIC

- CONTRACTING COURSE ADVANCED
- BUSINESS PROGRAM MANAGERS (REC/F&H)
- BUSINESS OPERATIONS MANAGEMENT (F&H)
- STRATEGIC BUSINESS PLANNING - COLLEGE OF WILLIAM AND MARY
- STRATEGIC RETAIL MANAGEMENT - COLLEGE OF WILLIAM AND MARY

WARRANT OFFICER/CHIEF WARRANT OFFICER
- EXECUTIVE SKILLS DEVELOPMENT
- MAKING MEETINGS WORK
- CONTRACTING COURSE BASIC
- CONTRACTING COURSE ADVANCED
- BUSINESS PROGRAM MANAGERS (REC/F&H)
- BUSINESS OPERATIONS MANAGEMENT (F&H)
- STRATEGIC BUSINESS PLANNING - COLLEGE OF WILLIAM AND MARY
- STRATEGIC RETAIL MANAGEMENT - COLLEGE OF WILLIAM AND MARY

MCCS T&R MANUAL

APPENDIX B

REFERENCES

29 CFR 1910.120	Occupational Safety and Health Standards - Hazardous Waste Operations and Emergency Response
DOD 5500.7R	Joint Ethics Regulation (JER)
DODD 1015.2	Military Morale, Welfare and Recreation
DODD 1330.9	Armed Services Exchange Regulations
DODD 4105.67	Non-appropriated Fun (NAF) Procurement Policy
DODD 7000.14	DOD Financial Management Policy and Procedure
DODI 1015.10	Programs for Military Morale, Welfare, and Recreation (MWR)
DODI 1015.14	Establishment, Management, and Control of Non-appropriated Fund Instrumentalities and Financial Management of Supporting Resources
DODI 4105.71	Non-appropriated Fun (NAF) Procurement
JP 1-0	Joint Doctrine for Personnel Support to Joint Operations
JP 3-07.5	Joint Tactics, Techniques, and Procedures for Noncombatant Evacuation
MCO 10120.28	Individual Clothing Regulations
MCO 10123.8	Commercially Procured Marine Corps Uniforms and Accessories Sold Through Marine Corps Exchanges
MCO 1700.22	Alcohol Beverage Control in the Marine Corps
MCO 5100.8	Marine Corps Occupational Safety and Health (OSH) Policy Order
MCO P12000.11	Marine Corps Non-appropriated Fund Personnel Policy Manual
MCO P1700.27	Marine Corps Community Services Policy Manual
MCO P1700.29	Marine Corps Semper Fit Program Manual
MCO P1700.30	Marine Corps Community Services Business Operations Manual
MCO P4066.17	Marine Corps Exchange Security and Loss Prevention Manual
MCO P4200.15	Marine Corps Purchasing Procedures Manual
MCO P4790.2	MIMMS Field Procedures Manual
MCO P5300.9	Marine Corps Non-appropriated Funds Instrumentalities Personnel Manual
MCO P7010.20	Marine Corps Community Services Non-appropriated Fund Procurement Policy
MCWP 4-1	Logistics Operations
MCWP 4-11	Tactical Level Logistics
MCWP 4-11.8	Services in an Expeditionary Environment
MCWO 4-12	Operations Level Logistics
NAVMC 2712	Marine Corps Club System Operations Manual
NAVMED P5010	Navy Sanitation
OPNAV 4000.84	Interservice and Intragovermental Support Program
NAVINST P5212.5	Disposal Navy/Marine Corps Records
SL 3-011362B	Tent GP Old Type SL-3
TM 10-8340-240-12	Tent GP Modular New Type TM

www.ingramcontent.com/pod-product-compliance
Lightning Source LLC
Chambersburg PA
CBHW081143290526
45795CB00006B/2347